Wolves in Sheep's Clothing: How to Spot Counterfeit Christians

Step-by-Step Guide To Helping Counterfeit Christians
Unmask the Masquerade

Theresa A Carson

Copyright Page

Dedication

This book is dedicated with love and gratitude to the Graves and Carson families. You are more than family to me—you are a constant source of strength, encouragement, and unwavering support. Words can hardly capture how much I love you all and how much you ~~mean~~ to me.

To my mother, Annie: Your generous heart and deep trust in God set the example that became the very foundation of my life. You showed me what it means to love selflessly, to walk in faith, and to trust God's plan, no matter the circumstances. You are the living example of grace, strength, and faith, and I will forever be grateful for the life lessons you've imparted.

To my late grandmother, Louise Graves: I can still feel the touch of your hands as you washed my feet, anointed me with oil, and spoke the powerful words of God over my life. Your faith was a light that guided me through my darkest times, and your prayers are woven into the fabric of my spirit. Though you are no longer here in body, your love and faith continue to live on in me, shaping every step I take.

In memory of Aunt Julia and Aunt Delmar: You two are the warrior women who instilled in me the desire to follow Christ with a full heart, and to always seek and honor God's assignment for my life. Your strength, wisdom, and commitment to faith have not only inspired me—they have shaped me into who I am today. I am blessed beyond measure to have had such powerful role models in my life.

I am also deeply grateful to Pastor Desiree and Jerome Joe of New Light Star Missionary Baptist Church. Through your ministry, you provided the keys used in this book. Your guidance and prayers have been instrumental in the creation of this book, and I will forever be thankful for the spiritual wisdom you shared with me.

To my beloved family at Word of Faith International Christian Center: You have been my rock through some of the most challenging yet faith-filled seasons of my life. Your love, prayers, and constant encouragement have lifted me up and carried me through. And to my extended family at Faith Food Bookstore: Your presence and support during this journey have been a testament to the power of community. You've been with me every step of the way, and I love you all deeply.

This book is not just a reflection of my work—it's a reflection of all of you. Your faith, love, and encouragement have been the foundation upon which this work was built. Thank you for being the incredible people you are, and for walking beside me as I've pursued the calling God placed on my life.

With love and deep appreciation, I dedicate this book to all of you. May God bless each and every one of you, as you've blessed me.

Table of Contents

Introduction

There's a unique joy that comes from sharing the gospel, especially when it involves something as precious as faith. I see this joy reflected in the eager faces of seniors at a local living facility. Every Saturday, a group of us gather—not just to learn but to connect and grow together through the teachings of the Bible.

I first stumbled upon this Bible study group while accompanying my mom, who had recently sold her condo and moved into an assisted living senior community. What started as a simple visit soon became a cornerstone of my spiritual journey. Little did I know that these gatherings would spark a transformation that continues to shape my life today.

The attendees of the Bible study come from diverse backgrounds—some stepping into a church-like setting for the first time, while others have spent a lifetime in the pews. Despite their differences, they all share a common thread: a hunger for knowledge and a deep desire to understand God's word.

The beauty of these gatherings lies not just in the lessons taught by Pastor Jerome Joe but also in the mutual inspiration shared between him and the participants. Pastor Joe often reminds us that teaching is a two-way street, where the exchange of wisdom and experiences enriches everyone involved. I find myself looking forward to these sessions, motivated by the anticipation and receptiveness of our group.

For those who have never attended a formal church service, the Bible study serves as a welcoming introduction to the Christian faith, offering a sense of community and belonging. For lifelong churchgoers, it provides a convenient way to continue spiritual education and reflection in a comfortable, familiar environment. Our Bible study group truly embodies a melting pot of faith and learning.

Each Saturday, the group brings together individuals from all walks of life, united by a shared desire to learn more about the Christian faith. These gatherings are not only for the devout who have spent years in church pews but also for those new to the Bible, seeking deeper understanding.

Our Bible study group is a beacon of light, providing a warm and inviting atmosphere where questions are encouraged and every opinion is valued. Under Pastor Joe's guidance, we explore Christianity without the formality of a traditional church service, making the experience more intimate and accessible—especially for seniors with physical challenges. For seasoned churchgoers, it's a chance to delve deeper into scripture and reflect meaningfully on their spiritual journeys.

Interpretations, discussions, and applications of lessons to daily life make our Bible study group a truly enriching experience. The diversity within the group, with members from various ethnic backgrounds and levels of biblical knowledge, adds depth and broadens perspectives on the teachings.

One of the most beautiful aspects of this group lies in its diversity. Some members can quote Bible verses by heart and share stories of a lifetime spent in the church, while others may not yet know the difference between the Old and New Testaments. This blend of knowledge and experience creates a dynamic environment where learning is reciprocal. Seasoned learners provide a solid foundation, while the fresh perspectives of newcomers spark new insights and passionate discussions.

For me, this group represents more than just fellowship. It's about creating and nurturing a space where faith can flourish, questions can be explored, and the love of God can be shared openly. The journey of sharing faith here serves as a powerful reminder of the impact one person can have when they lead with love and a passion for spreading the gospel.

Attending this Bible study group has given me countless memorable moments that resonate long after the sessions end.

One of the most heartwarming experiences is witnessing a new attendee, someone who has never been part of a formal church service, begin to understand and connect with the teachings of the Bible. The look of realization and joy on their face is a profound testament to the power of faith and the importance of sharing God's love.

Another impactful moment occurs when a long-time churchgoer shares a deeply personal story that brings scripture to life. These moments create a sense of community and connection among group members, as they see the real-world application of their faith. For the newcomers, it offers a glimpse of what it means to have a personal relationship with the Father.

Perhaps the most moving experiences arise during times of loss or hardship when the group collectively finds comfort and solace in the scriptures. The shared strength and unity that emerge during these moments form an unbreakable bond within the group.

Equally memorable are the spontaneous discussions, where attendees eagerly ask questions and engage in deep theological conversations. These exchanges reflect the group's hunger for knowledge and their active engagement with the Word of God.

One particularly striking discussion arose from a question about living a Christian lifestyle: "Why are there so many hypocrites in church?" This sparked a profound dialogue about carnal and counterfeit Christians, shedding light on the contrast between genuine faith and outward appearances. The discussion highlighted how encounters with insincere Christians can deter some people from church, yet also emphasized the importance of focusing on a personal relationship with God rather than the imperfections of others.

The question of hypocrisy within church communities is a deeply emotional and challenging one, touching on the very essence of what it means to live a life of faith. It's a concern often voiced not only by those outside the church but also by those within its walls—

individuals who long for a community that truly reflects the values they hold dear.

Hypocrisy, or the perception of it, along with fake and carnal Christians, can indeed be a stumbling block for many. It raises pressing questions about authenticity and the genuine practice of faith. When people witness a disconnect between preached values and lived realities, it can lead to disillusionment and hesitancy in engaging with the church.

For several months, our Bible study group delved deeply into scripture, seeking to understand the true nature of belief and the character of a genuine believer. It all began with a question about hypocrisy in the church, which sparked a journey of exploring what it means to be a true follower of God the Father and a recipient of the sacrifice of Jesus Christ. This discussion about carnal, or fake Christians, inspired me to embark on this writing journey and pen this mini-book. My goal is to support individuals in their Christian walk by offering guidance, insight, and encouragement. I hope this book helps readers deepen their faith, navigate spiritual challenges, and grow in their relationship with God the Father.

Our study and reflections have been profoundly eye-opening. Through God's word, we have discovered that the characteristics of a true believer are transformative and evident in one's actions and choices. True belief isn't just a title one claims—it is a continuous, living expression of faith and growth.

Being a believer is about walking in the light, demonstrating love to others, and embodying the teachings of Christ in daily life. It isn't about outward displays like bumper stickers on a car or oversized pins proclaiming one's faith. Instead, the presence of a true believer should naturally change the atmosphere and be reflected in their character. A genuine believer is a ray of light in a dark room, illuminating the way for others through their example.

We are living in what the Bible calls the end of days—a time shrouded in both fear and great anticipation. As the prophetic words of ancient scripture echo through the tumultuous events of our present, it feels as though we are witnessing the grand tapestry of fate being woven before our very eyes. Natural disasters ravage the earth with unprecedented fury, wars rage with unrelenting cruelty, and moral decay spreads like an uncontainable plague, all heralding a profound spiritual reckoning. Mass shootings have sadly become commonplace in America. Recently, we endured several years of an unprecedented global pandemic, losing millions of lives to the devastating disease known as COVID-19. In this era of heightened urgency, humanity stands on the precipice, teetering between redemption and ruin. The signs are clear, and the message is undeniable: this is not a moment to be taken lightly. The Bible prophecy we read and meditate on is coming to life before our very eyes.

In recent years, we've been captivated by an extraordinary array of lunar events, including record numbers of moon phases, spectacular blue moons, and mesmerizing super moons. These celestial phenomena have graced our night skies with breathtaking beauty, reminding us of the ever-changing nature of the cosmos. The most recent eclipse was a total solar eclipse that occurred on April 8, 2024.

(Amos 8:9)

And it shall come to pass in that day, saith the Lord GOD, that I will cause the sun to go down at noon, and I will darken the earth in the clear day.

Many Christian prophets warn that a solar eclipse is considered a special event because it is seen as a symbolic representation of divine judgment. Some modern-day prophets say the eclipse could foreshadow "the end times," the second coming of Christ as described in scripture.

(Luke 21:25-28)

And there shall be signs in the sun, and in the moon, and in the stars; and upon the earth distress of nations, with perplexity; the sea and the waves roaring; Men's hearts failing them for fear, and for looking after those things which are coming on the earth: for the powers of heaven shall be shaken. And then shall they see the Son of man coming in a cloud with power and great glory. And when these things begin to come to pass, then look up, and lift up your heads; for your redemption draweth nigh.

(Joel 2:30-31)

And I will shew wonders in the heavens and in the earth, blood, and fire, and pillars of smoke. The sun shall be turned into darkness, and the moon into blood, before the great and the terrible day of the LORD come.

(Acts 2:19-21)

And I will shew wonders in heaven above, and signs in the earth beneath; blood, and fire, and vapour of smoke: The sun shall be turned into darkness, and the moon into blood, before that great and notable day of the Lord come: And it shall come to pass, that whosoever shall call on the name of the Lord shall be saved.

It's a dramatic and sobering reminder that our choices now bear eternal consequences. Now is not the time to be a lukewarm or counterfeit believer. The end of days calls us to awaken from any spiritual slumber, idleness, or laziness. Now is the time to seek God's truth with fervor and to embrace the hope and salvation offered by faith. It's a pivotal moment in the cosmic narrative, urging us to face our destiny with reverence, resolve, and an unyielding quest to discover our divine purpose. In this time and season, you must know your God assignment.

As we delved into the scriptures, it became very clear that God's word revealed to us that many who identify as believers may just pose as counterfeit Christians. This realization has been both challenging and humbling, prompting us to reflect on our own lives and the authenticity of our faith. Many people are unaware of the profound dangers and spiritual repercussions of living as a counterfeit Christian. By understanding these risks, we can fully appreciate the importance of genuine faith and transformation in our lives. God expects us to warn our brothers and sisters of the faith that danger lies ahead for those pretenders.

I believe we are living in the end times, and now more than ever, it is crucial to abandon any pretense and live as genuine Christians. The stakes are too high to live a counterfeit lifestyle. The decision that defines your eternal destiny hinges upon the manner in which you conduct your faith and character life for Christ. This is a time for deep reflection and sincere commitment to our faith. We must strive to embody the teachings of Christ in every aspect of our lives—from our interactions with others to our personal spiritual practices. The urgency of the times calls for a wholehearted dedication to living out our beliefs authentically and with integrity. We have received our orders to preach the gospel to every creature.

(Mark 16:15-16)

And he said unto them, Go ye into all the world, and preach the gospel to every creature. He that believeth and is baptized shall be saved; but he that believeth not shall be damned.

The Great Pretenders: Understanding Counterfeit Christians

The term "counterfeit Christian" describes someone who may outwardly display characteristics or behaviors associated with Christianity but whose beliefs and actions do not align with the core teachings of God's Word. The idea of a counterfeit Christian is linked to the concern that some individuals may possess a superficial or insincere commitment to the faith. While this may be a shocking concept to some, it can manifest in various ways—such as adhering to the rituals and traditions of the church without cultivating a genuine personal conviction or relationship with God. It might also involve publicly espousing Christian values while privately engaging in unethical or non-Christian behavior.

The goal is not to judge others but to encourage believers to examine their own faith, ensuring it is genuine and rooted in the teachings of Christ. A true believer must be vigilant in their spiritual journey, striving for authenticity rather than imitating outward signs of Christianity without embracing its core principles. The term "counterfeit" implies deception or falseness, suggesting that one might appear faithful outwardly while lacking a true inner transformation.

Moreover, the emphasis on avoiding ignorance highlights the importance of knowledge and understanding in one's spiritual life. Ignorance can lead to a superficial practice of Christianity, where individuals follow rituals and traditions without understanding their deeper significance. To combat this, believers are encouraged to seek knowledge, ask questions, and engage in meaningful discussions about their faith. God has provided resources for our growth.

(Ephesians 4:11-16)

And he gave some, apostles; and some, prophets; and some, evangelists; and some, pastors and teachers; For the perfecting of the saints, for the work of the ministry, for the edifying of the body of Christ: Till we all come in the unity of the faith, and of the knowledge of the Son of God, unto a perfect man, unto the measure of the stature of the fulness of Christ: That we henceforth be no more children, tossed to and fro, and carried about with every wind of doctrine, by the sleight of men, and cunning craftiness, whereby they lie in wait to deceive; But speaking the truth in love, may grow up into him in all things, which is the head, even Christ: From whom the whole body fitly joined together and compacted by that which every joint supplieth, according to the effectual working in the measure of every part, maketh increase of the body unto the edifying of itself in love.

The message conveyed by the phrase "counterfeit Christian" is not one of judgment but a call for self-examination and spiritual growth. True Christianity involves a deep, personal commitment to living according to Christ's teachings. Believers are encouraged to look beyond outward appearances and focus on nurturing an authentic relationship with God. This approach fosters a faith that is resilient, informed, and reflective of the transformative power of Christian beliefs.

Counterfeit:

1. To forge; to copy or imitate, without authority or right, and with a view to deceive or defraud, by passing the copy or thing forged, for that which is original or genuine; as, to *counterfeit* a seal, a bond, To make a likeness or resemblance of anything with a view to defraud.
2. To imitate; to copy; to make or put on a resemblance; as, to *counterfeit* the voice of another person; to *counterfeit* piety. (from the American Dictionary of the English Language, published by Noah Webster in 1828)

"Counterfeit Christians" are those who outwardly display faith yet lack genuine commitment or integrity in their beliefs and actions. They wear the façade of piety, but their hearts and deeds tell a different story. Think of them as actors on a stage, playing the role of a devout believer without true conviction. In many cases, this is someone who knows the rituals and language of faith, but their actions and character reveal a lack of true belief.

They live without fear or reverence for God, their hearts devoid of genuine faith in His existence. Their lives are marked by a profound spiritual void—a detachment from the divine that leaves them wandering aimlessly in darkness. Tragically, most do not even realize they are living in deception. They are unaware that their lives are offensive in the very nostrils of God.

(Psalm 14:1)

The fool hath said in his heart, there is no God. They are corrupt, they have done abominable works, there is none that doeth good.

The Hidden Dangers of Living Your Life as a Counterfeit Christian:

1. Self-Deception

A counterfeit Christian may believe they are saved or in right standing with God because of external behaviors—such as attending church, performing good deeds, or engaging in charitable acts—but lack true faith in Christ. This creates a false sense of security, assuming that outward actions alone are sufficient to be accepted by God. Scripture warns against this:

(Matthew 7:21-23)

Not everyone who says to me, 'Lord, Lord,' will enter the kingdom of heaven, but the one who does the will of my Father who is in heaven. Many will say to me in that day, Lord, Lord, have we not prophesied in thy name? and in thy name have cast out devils? and in thy name done many wonderful works? And then will I profess unto them, I never knew you: depart from me, ye that work iniquity.

2. Spiritual Stagnation

Have you ever felt like your journey with Christ has hit a standstill? Do you yearn for deeper growth and meaning? Perhaps you find yourself scrolling through social media or online shopping during church services, instead of engaging in the message, praise, or worship. You glance at others and think, "It really doesn't take all that." But the truth is—it does. It takes all that and more. True Believers desire to do life together.

(Hebrews 10:24-25)

And let us consider one another to provoke unto love and to good works: Not forsaking the assembling of ourselves together, as the manner of some is; but exhorting one another: and so much the more, as ye see the day approaching. We do it all unto the Lord Jesus Christ because we are grateful. Grateful for the joy of the Lord, peace, security, prosperity, health and most importantly forgiveness of our sins and eternal life. We learned that this faith walk is through God and that's how we live an authentic Christian life.

Without a true relationship with Christ, a counterfeit Christian will inevitably experience spiritual stagnation and emptiness. Genuine faith fosters spiritual growth, transformation, and intimacy with God. Without a connection to the Holy Ghost, spiritual life becomes

[14]

nothing more than hollow routines, devoid of the fruits of the Spirit—such as love, joy, peace, patience, and more.

Some root causes of spiritual stagnation include pride, self-sufficiency, complacency, laziness, and a struggle with stillness or quietness. Spiritually stagnant individuals often expect God to do all the work for them, failing to recognize the importance of active participation and intentional effort in their walk with God.

(2 Timothy 3:5)

Having a form of godliness, but denying the power thereof: from such turn away.

And it shall come to pass at that time, that I will search Jerusalem with candles, and punish the men that are settled on their lees: that say in their heart, The LORD will not do good, neither will he do evil. **(Zephaniah 1:12)** God will punish those who were stagnant in spirit, or became spiritually complacent.

3. Leading Others Astray

Counterfeit Christians can have a negative influence on others. Their lack of authenticity may discourage others from seeking genuine faith. If someone is pretending to live by Christian principles but their life reflects selfishness, deceit, or hypocrisy, it can damage the credibility of the faith and lead others away from the truth. (Matthew 18:6) says that anyone who tempts a believer to sin, will be judged harshly. The Bible warns that a counterfeit believer in Jesus that has caused another to stumble, or be led astray or to sin, God himself will judge one day. Those people who are leaders that misuse his word will be judged more harshly.

(Matthew 23:13-14)

But woe unto you, scribes and Pharisees, hypocrites! for ye shut up the kingdom of heaven against men: for ye neither go in yourselves, neither suffer ye them that are entering to go in. Woe Unto you, scribes and Pharisees, hypocrites! for ye devour widows' houses, and for a pretence make long prayer: therefore ye shall receive the greater damnation.

(2 Peter 2:1)

But there were false prophets also among the people, even as there shall be false teachers among you, who privily shall bring in damnable heresies, even denying the Lord that bought them, and bring upon themselves swift destruction.

4. Ineffective Witness

A counterfeit Christian's witness to the world is deeply compromised. Without a genuine transformation of the heart, their actions fail to reflect Christ's love, mercy, or humility. This inconsistency can become a stumbling block for those seeking truth or looking to Christianity for hope, as they may be disheartened by the lack of authenticity in the counterfeit Christian's life.

(Matthew 5:16)

In the same way, let your light shine before others, that they may see your good deeds and glorify your Father in heaven.

(Luke 9:26)

For whosoever shall be ashamed of me and of my words, of him shall the Son of man be ashamed, when he shall come in his own glory, and in his Father's, and of the holy angels.

(Matthew 10:33)

But whosoever shall deny me before men, him will I also deny before my Father which is in heaven.

5. Facing Judgment

I firmly believe that carnal Christians live this way because they struggle to truly grasp and believe in the existence of God. It's not merely a lack of faith; rather, they have no faith, nor fear or reverence for God. In their minds, God does not exist, so they perceive no repercussions for their evil deeds or actions. They mistake God's continued mercy for an absence of judgment, using it to justify their ongoing life of sin.

Whether you believe it or not, we were designed to live in eternal kingdoms. The choice is yours: eternal life with God or eternal separation in hell with Satan and his angels. God loves you enough to grant you the freedom to make your own life decisions, but those decisions have eternal consequences.

Genuine faith and belief in the sacrifice of Jesus Christ is the only path to salvation. Those who merely "play the part" without sincere belief or repentance will face God's judgment, as they are not truly reconciled to Him.

(Matthew 25:11-12)

Afterward came also the other virgins, saying, Lord, Lord, open to us. But he answered and said, Verily I say unto you, I know you not.

(Luke 13:25)

When once the master of the house is risen up, and hath shut to the door, and ye begin to stand without, and to knock at the door, saying, Lord, Lord, open unto us; and he shall answer and say unto you, I know you not whence ye are:

(Matthew 7:21-23)

Not every one that saith unto me, Lord, Lord, shall enter into the kingdom of heaven; but he that doeth the will of my Father which is in heaven. Many will say to me in that day, Lord, Lord, have we not prophesied in thy name? and in thy name have cast out devils? and in thy name done many wonderful works? And then will I profess unto them, I never knew you: depart from me, ye that work iniquity.

6. Living in Hypocrisy

Hypocrisy often stems from a lack of genuine fear and reverence for God. When individuals fail to grasp or respect God's holiness, they are more prone to fall into the trap of living a double life. This disconnect not only harms their relationship with God but also diminishes their ability to fully experience His grace, peace, and guidance.

Living authentically—with a sincere reverence for God—ensures that actions align with beliefs, fostering a deeper and more meaningful spiritual journey. It's vital to reflect on this and commit to genuine devotion in every aspect of life.

A Counterfeit Christian risk living a double life. Outwardly, they may appear faithful and righteous, but inwardly, they wrestle with sin, doubts, selfish motives, and even psychological stress or anxiety. This inner conflict leads to guilt and profound emotional turmoil, as

[19]

they struggle with authenticity before God, themselves, and others. Living in hypocrisy is, ultimately, living under the heavy burden of sin and unresolved guilt.

(Matthew 23:27)

Woe unto you, scribes and Pharisees, hypocrites! for ye are like unto whited sepulchres, which indeed appear beautiful outward, but are within full of dead men's bones, and of all uncleanness.

(Matthew 23:28)

Even so ye also outwardly appear righteous unto men, but within ye are full of hypocrisy and iniquity.

(1 Kings 18:21)

And Elijah came unto all the people, and said, How long halt ye between two opinions? if the LORD be God, follow him: but if Baal, then follow him. And the people answered him not a word.

(James 1:7)

That man should not expect to receive anything from the Lord.

7. Missed Relationship with God

The most tragic danger of being a counterfeit Christian is missing out on the relationship with God that lies at the heart of Christianity. True faith offers a personal and transformative connection with

God through Jesus Christ—a relationship filled with peace, joy, and purpose. However, a counterfeit Christian, consumed by appearances or merely adhering to rules, misses this vital connection. As a result, they live without the comfort, guidance, and power of God's presence in their life.

(Matthew 15:8)

This people draweth nigh unto me with their mouth, and honoureth me with their lips; but their heart is far from me.

(Mark 7:6)

He answered and said unto them, Well hath Esaias prophesied of you hypocrites, as it is written, This people honoureth me with their lips, but their heart is far from me.

(Ezekiel 33:31)

And they come unto thee as the people cometh, and they sit before thee as my people, and they hear thy words, but they will not do them: for with their mouth they shew much love, but their heart goeth after their covetousness.

A missed relationship with God results in a permanent state of separation from His love and grace. In essence, being a counterfeit Christian is dangerous because it replaces true faith with a superficial version of Christianity, leading to spiritual emptiness, an ineffective witness, and potentially eternal separation from God. The Bible calls for sincerity in faith and warns against the dangers of hypocrisy, emphasizing the importance of a real, transformative relationship with God.

Consider the tragedy of many people who attend church week after week, assuming they are saved, yet face the possibility of spending eternity in hell. As Jesus warned:

(Matthew 13:41-43)

The Son of man shall send forth his angels, and they shall gather out of his kingdom all things that offend, and them which do iniquity; And shall cast them into a furnace of fire: there shall be wailing and gnashing of teeth. Then shall the righteous shine forth as the sun in the kingdom of their Father. Who hath ears to hear, let him hear.

"Faith in Disguise: Tales of Counterfeit Christians"

Sister Busy Bee's Summer Salvation:

If asked, "When did you make Jesus Christ Lord of your life?" she would say it was during the sun-drenched days of yesteryear, amidst the quiet country life of South Carolina. "I think it was around the tender age of nine or ten," she'd declare, with the confidence of someone who just found their favorite sock after a perilous laundry expedition.

"I remember it vividly... I think," she'd add with a smile. It was during one of her many summer sojourns to visit her mom's great-aunt Ethel, a woman whose house was as grand and beautiful as her heart, and whose garden was the stuff of legend—and salad bowls.

Each morning, Sister Busy Bee awoke not to the blaring traffic and sirens of home but to a symphony of sizzling. Breakfast in Aunt Ethel's kitchen was a feast fit for royalty, with heavenly aromas wafting through the air—homemade biscuits, cinnamon rolls, and the pièce de résistance: Aunt Ethel's famous banana pudding. The kitchen, a temple of taste, was where hearts and appetites alike were filled.

Aunt Ethel was no ordinary woman; she was a pillar of the church, a beacon of faith (and flour). She led the women's group with the grace of a swan and the precision of a military general. Her Bible study sessions were renowned as places of healing, laughter, and profound learning of the Word. Aunt Ethel's deep connection to her faith was legendary. Rising before anyone else in the house, she'd spend the early morning hours reading scripture, praying, and singing praises to God. It was said she had daily conversations with the Holy Spirit.

It was in this environment of unwavering faith and flaky pastries that Sister Busy Bee found salvation. Watching Aunt Ethel in action was like attending a masterclass in devotion. "Yep, that's when I got saved," she'd say, recalling how Aunt Ethel would speak to God through scripture, prayer, and a symphony of worship that seemed capable of inspiring even the angels.

Now, Sister Busy Bee admits that she's much too busy to frequent church as often as her great-aunt did, but she tries to make it at least one Sunday out of the month—a testament to the lasting impact of those formative summer days. She still has the Bible Aunt Ethel gave her, though it remains in its original wrapping paper, with the book tabs taped to the front as if waiting patiently for the moment it will truly be unwrapped and embraced.

"But yeah, I know I'm saved because I went to church seven days a week during the summer with Auntie Ethel," she concludes, a smile on her face and the echo of hymns in her heart.

Sister Busy Bee, however, is much too busy for church these days. She works six days a week to maintain her lavish lifestyle, and Sunday has become her sacred day—of self-care. It's the one day she gets to sleep in, enjoy a manicure, pedicure, and steam facial. It's also the day she loves shopping at antique markets. Sister Busy Bee firmly believes that mimicking Auntie Ethel's faith-filled lifestyle earns her the right to salvation and eternal life, despite her lack of genuine spiritual engagement.

The Curious Case of Sister Mean Jean

Sister Mean Jean—known fondly (and fearfully) as Sister MJ—has over 40 years of service in the house of the Lord. She's a fixture in the church's landscape, a woman whose dedication is as unwavering as the Sunday sermon. Sister MJ has worn many hats: choir member, women's ministry participant, missionary, usher, and even the pastor's office assistant. Her commitment is legendary, her presence constant, and her hard work unquestionable.

But there's a twist to this tale of devotion.

Despite her faithfulness to the church, Sister MJ harbors a spirit spicier than the church potluck's infamous chili. She's as mean as a rattlesnake on a hot summer day, with a bite to match her bark. She's the living embodiment of the adage, "Forgive and forget? Not in this lifetime!"

Sister MJ's memory is a steel trap, particularly when it comes to grievances. To err is human, to forgive is divine, but Sister MJ seems to have skipped that lesson. She holds grudges with a vice-like grip, and she's not shy about letting people know it. Ask her what she despises most, and she'll answer without hesitation: "People. I hate people."

It's a jarring statement from someone so deeply entrenched in the house of the Lord. For Sister MJ, **Leviticus 19:18** seems more like a suggestion than a commandment: *"Thou shalt not avenge, nor bear any grudge against the children of thy people, but thou shalt love thy neighbour as thyself: I am the LORD."*

Her actions and attitude serve as a cautionary tale about the danger of faithfully serving in God's house without letting His word transform the heart.

Reflections in the Mirror: A Step-by-Step Journey of Self-Examination

Examination:

The act of examining; a careful search or inquiry, with a view to discover truth or the real state of things. A careful and accurate inspection of a thing and its parts

(Hosea 4:6)

My people are destroyed for lack of knowledge: because thou hast rejected knowledge, I will also reject thee, that thou shalt be no priest to me: seeing thou hast forgotten the law of thy God, I will also forget thy children.

In the narrative, the characters have willfully turned their backs on God, casting aside the sacred teachings of Jesus. Lost in a spiritual wilderness, they have succumbed to the seductive idols of their own creation: the deities of unforgiveness, arrogance, resentment, greed, wealth, malice, and obliviousness. These false idols, forged from the darkest facets of human nature, now command their devotion, leading them further into the abyss of spiritual decay. Tragically, neither of them recognizes their perilous state.

There are only two natures operating in the earth: the nature of God and that of the Devil. God will honor your choice regarding whom you will follow, give your heart to, and lend your ear.

(2 Corinthians 13:5)

Examine yourselves, whether ye be in the faith; prove your own selves. Know ye not your own selves, how that Jesus Christ is in you, except ye be reprobates?

(Lamentations 3:40)

Let us search and try our ways, and turn again to the LORD.

(1 Corinthians 11:28)

But let a man examine himself, and so let him eat of the bread, and drink of the cup.

The call for self-examination is a critical aspect of avoiding counterfeit Christianity. It is a process in which individuals assess their beliefs, actions, and motivations to ensure they align with the teachings of Christ. This introspective practice is essential because it helps believers identify areas where they may have strayed from their faith. It also provides an opportunity to realign with authentic Christian values, fostering spiritual growth and renewal.

God expects true believers to dedicate time to self-reflection and personal growth. These practices are vital components of spiritual development. As believers, taking the time to introspect and seek a deeper understanding of God can lead to a more fulfilling life and a closer connection with the Father. This process involves examining God's character, motives, actions, and promises while also striving to align oneself with His will. As Kingdom Citizens, we should actively seek ways to grow and improve in the Lord. This journey fosters greater self-awareness and harmony with the Father, Son, and Holy Spirit. It requires asking tough questions, being honest about the answers, and making necessary adjustments to live a life pleasing to God.

Lifestyle examination is another essential practice. It involves assessing daily habits and routines to determine whether they contribute to a fulfilling, God-centered life. This could include evaluating time spent in God's Word, your prayer life, and other areas like diet, exercise, work-life balance, and social interactions. The goal is to identify areas for improvement, ensuring that these practices lead to a more balanced and God-honoring lifestyle.

Those who claim to know the Lord but show no evidence of transformation in their lives should honestly question whether they have truly been born again. The question posed in Bible study about hypocrisy or counterfeit Christians reflects the widespread sin that has infiltrated the Church today. It's a sobering thought: how many people attending church or professing to follow Christ are not genuinely born again?

If someone is truly born of God, can they continue living in blatant sin, unchanged in actions or attitudes? Consider this: Do you truly confess Jesus Christ as your Lord and Savior? Do you curse, steal, cheat, lie, bear false witness, harbor jealousy, struggle with anger, or refuse to forgive others? These behaviors are inconsistent with the characteristics of a born-again believer and a child of God.

We must take the time to learn and embody the character and nature of God, allowing His transformative power to renew our hearts and lives.

God is Love: Living in His Light: Embracing the Gift of Salvation

Will a loving God send someone to hell? The answer is no. The decision to enter hell is a choice that each individual must make. God has granted us free will, and the decision to believe in Him and walk in His ways is entirely up to us. God has made His truth available to everyone.

(Romans 1:20)

"For the invisible things of Him from the creation of the world are clearly seen, being understood by the things that are made, even His eternal power and Godhead; so that they are without excuse."

(John 3:18-20)

"He that believeth on Him is not condemned: but he that believeth not is condemned already, because he hath not believed in the name of the only begotten Son of God. And this is the condemnation, that light is come into the world, and men loved darkness rather than light, because their deeds were evil. For every one that doeth evil hateth the light, neither cometh to the light, lest his deeds should be reproved."

Our choices have eternal consequences.

Living Truth: The Core Attributes of Authentic Christians Who Walk the Talk and the Mark of a Genuine Disciple

John 3:3-6

Jesus answered and said unto him, "Verily, verily, I say unto thee, Except a man be born again, he cannot see the kingdom of God." Nicodemus saith unto him, "How can a man be born when he is old? Can he enter the second time into his mother's womb, and be born?" Jesus answered, "Verily, verily, I say unto thee, Except a man be born of water and of the Spirit, he cannot enter into the kingdom of God. That which is born of the flesh is flesh; and that which is born of the Spirit is spirit."

Romans 10:9

"That if thou shalt confess with thy mouth the Lord Jesus, and shalt believe in thine heart that God hath raised Him from the dead, thou shalt be saved. For with the heart man believeth unto righteousness, and with the mouth confession is made unto salvation."

1 Corinthians 12:3

"Wherefore I give you to understand, that no man speaking by the Spirit of God calleth Jesus accursed: and that no man can say that Jesus is the Lord, but by the Holy Ghost."

Salvation means deliverance and redemption from death and separation from God. When Adam was given the keys to authority by God in the Garden of Eden and disobeyed by handing the authority over to Satan, it caused the fall of man, spiritual death, and separation from God. Our loving Creator, full of mercy, desired for us to spend eternity in heaven, rather than hell, which was created for the devil and his angels. God loves us so much that He sent His only Son, Jesus, who bore the punishment for our sins that justice demanded.

The restoration of man is a free gift and requires a choice. If you said YES, the divine seed is planted in you. That seed will change your very nature, and the renewed Spirit will be one with God the Father. God's very nature and life will be reproduced within you. You are now Born Again. The old sin nature, once inside of you, will become disturbed and will detest everything evil. Your desires and tastes will begin to change. The sooner you leave behind the Babylonian system and the world's way of doing things, the better. You are now in a new Kingdom, and your citizenship was bought and paid for by the blood of Christ.

Exploring the Authentic Characteristics That Define a True Follower of Christ

The authentic characteristics that define a true follower of Christ involves delving into several core attributes.

Steps to Embody True Discipleship:

Are You Living the Truth? Do You Embody the Core Attributes of Authentic Christians Who Walk the Talk?

The Mark of a Genuine Disciple:

1. Hear God's Voice.

(John 18:37) *Pilate therefore said unto him, Art thou a king then? Jesus answered, Thou sayest that I am a king. To this end was I born, and for this cause came I into the world, that I should bear witness unto the truth. Everyone that is of the truth heareth   my   voice.* (John 10:27) *My sheep hear my voice, and I know them, and they follow me.*

2. Born-again People Have Christ Living Within.

(Galatians 2:20) *I am crucified with Christ: nevertheless I live; yet not I, but Christ liveth in me: and the life which I now live in the flesh I live by the faith of the Son of God, who loved me, and gave himself for me.*

(Colossians 1:27) *To whom God would make known what is*

[34]

the riches of the glory of this mystery among the Gentiles; which is Christ in you, the hope of glory.

3. Believers Have Sound Minds.

(Philippians 2:5-6) *Let this mind be in you, which was also in Christ Jesus, who, being in the form of God, did not consider it not robbery to be equal with God:*

(2 Corinthians 2:16) *"For who has known the mind of the Lord, so as to instruct Him?" But we have the mind of Christ.*

4. Born-again People Have the Gift of Speaking in Tongues and Have the Ability to Interpret What Has Been Spoken.

When you speak in tongues, it is a language not naturally acquired but supernaturally given by the Holy Spirit.

(Mark 16:17) *And these signs will accompany those who believe: In My name, they will drive out demons; they will speak in new tongues.*

(Acts 2:4) *And they were all filled with the Holy Ghost, and began to speak with other tongues, as the Spirit gave them utterance.*

(1 Corinthians 12:10) *To another the working of miracles; to another prophecy; to another discerning of spirits; to another divers kinds of tongues; to another the interpretation of tongues.*

(Acts 19:6) *And when Paul had laid his hands upon them, the Holy Ghost came on them; and they spake with tongues, and prophesied.*

5. Righteous in Christ.

(1 John 2:29) *If ye know that he is righteous, ye know that every one that doeth righteousness is born of him.*

(Philippians 1:11) *Filled with the fruit of righteousness that comes through Jesus Christ, to the glory and praise of God.*

(1 John 3:7) *Little children, let no man deceive you: he that doeth righteousness is righteous, even as he is righteous.*

6. Do not commit sin or practice a sinful lifestyle.

(1 John 3:5-10) *"And ye know that he was manifested to take away our sins; and in him is no sin. Whosoever abideth in him sinneth not: whosoever sinneth hath not seen him, neither known him. Little children, let no man deceive you: he that doeth righteousness is righteous, even as he is righteous. He that committeth sin is of the devil; for the devil sinneth from the beginning. For this purpose, the Son of God was manifested, that he might destroy the works of the devil. Whosoever is born of God doth not commit sin; for his seed remaineth in him: and he cannot sin, because he is born of God. In this, the children of God are manifest, and the children of the devil: whosoever doeth not righteousness is not of God, neither he that loveth not his brother."*

7. Confess and believe that Jesus is Lord.

(Romans 10:9-10) *"That if thou shalt confess with thy mouth the Lord Jesus, and shalt believe in thine heart that God hath raised him from the dead, thou shalt be saved. For with the heart man believeth unto righteousness; and with the mouth confession is made unto salvation."*

(John 3:16) *"For God so loved the world that He gave His one and only Son, that everyone who believes in Him shall not perish but have eternal life."*

(1 John 3:16) *"Hereby perceive we the love of God, because he laid down his life for us: and we ought to lay down our lives for the brethren."*

8. Born-again people keep His commandments.

(1 John 5:3) *"For this is the love of God, that we keep His commandments: and His commandments are not grievous."*

(Psalm 112:1) *"Hallelujah! Blessed is the man who fears the LORD, who greatly delights in His commandments."*

(Proverbs 3:1-2) *"My son, forget not my law; but let thine heart keep my commandments: For length of days, and long life, and peace, shall they add to thee."*

9. Overcomers, who have overcome this world.

(1 John 5:4) *"For whatsoever is born of God overcometh* the world: and this is the victory that overcometh the world, even our faith."

(Philippians 4:13) *"I can do all things through Christ through Christ which strengtheneth me." (Romans 8:37) "Nay, in all these things we are more than conquerors through him that loved us."*

10.   Protected from the evil one.

(1 John 5:18) *"We know that whosoever is born of God sinneth not; but he that is begotten of God keepeth himself, and that wicked one toucheth him not."*

(2 Thessalonians 3:3) *"But the Lord is faithful, who shall stablish you, and keep you from evil."*

(2 Timothy 4:18) *"And the Lord will rescue me from every evil action and bring me safely into His heavenly kingdom. To Him be the glory forever and ever. Amen."*

11.   Genuinely Love Others and Are Not Mean or Evil.

(John 13:34-35) *"A new commandment I give to you, that you love one another; as I have loved you, that you also love one another. By this, all will know that you are My disciples, if you have love for one another."*

Born-again people want to do life together with other believers. They are by no means loners but truly desire to be in the company of other believers. Loving others is the master key to it all.

12. Have the Peace of God and No Fear.

(John 14:27) *"Peace I leave with you, My peace I give unto you: not as the world giveth, give I unto you. Let not your heart be troubled, neither let it be afraid."*
(2 Thessalonians 3:16) *"Now the Lord of peace Himself give you peace always by all means. The Lord be with you all."*
(Psalm 29:11) *"The LORD will give strength unto His people; the LORD will bless His people with peace."*

13. Born-Again People Do Not Seek Guidance from Astrology or the Occult.

I feel compelled to delve deeply into the subject of occult practices within the church. I frequently come across social media pages of individuals who profess to be Christians, yet they treat astrology as their gospel and source of guidance. This troubling trend needs to be addressed with urgency and clarity.

Do you confess Yeshua as your Lord and Savior? Born-again believers do not seek guidance from astrology or the occult. It astonishes me that the number of people who profess Yeshua as their Lord and Savior still engage in occult practices. As a believer, I have declared that Yeshua is Lord over my life. A Lord is someone with power, authority, or influence—a master or ruler. The Word of God clearly states that all wisdom, knowledge, and understanding come from Him.

You are a masterpiece, crafted by the very breath of God. You are a one-of-a-kind original, unparalleled in every way. No one else in the universe has your iris, your fingerprint, your footprint, your voice pattern, your life experiences, or the exact number of hairs on your head. You are a divine creation, fearfully and wonderfully made, with a purpose and a destiny that only you can fulfill through God. Embrace your uniqueness, for you are a precious and irreplaceable gem in the eyes of the Creator.

For a born-again believer to give power and authority to astrology goes directly against God's Word. The Lord calls involvement with the occult an abomination and detestable. God created us to be fearfully and wonderfully made, unique and awesome creations by His hand, in His image and likeness. He has given you His name and adopted you into His family, making you royalty, a Kingdom citizen. Why would you allow the devil to put a ring in your nose and lead you by a birth month? The devil assigns a relatability of personality traits associated with a birth sign. The whole premise of an astrological sign is that you are not unique, but are a part of a similar group. Your true birthday is the day you accepted Jesus Christ as your Lord and Savior, not the day you entered the world as a sinner in need of salvation.

Astrology originates from the occult practice of fortune-telling, where celestial entities like stars and planets were used to predict a person's past, present, and future. As a child of God, you are a unique individual, a joint heir, and a King's descendant. Christians are prohibited from seeking guidance from astrology, zodiac signs, tarot cards, readers, soothsayers, crystals, mediums, and channelers. Embrace your divine identity and reject these practices that diminish your true worth and connection to God.

This is what God's Word has to say about practicing the occult:

(Deuteronomy 18:9-14) *"When thou art come into the land which the LORD thy God giveth thee, thou shalt not learn to do after the abominations of those nations. There shall not be found among you any one that maketh his son or his daughter to pass through the fire, or that useth divination, or an observer of times, or an enchanter, or a witch, or a charmer, or a consulter with familiar spirits, or a wizard, or a necromancer. For all that do these things are an abomination unto the LORD: and because of these abominations the LORD thy God doth drive them out from before thee. Thou shalt be perfect with the LORD thy God. For these nations, which thou shalt possess, hearkened unto observers of times, and unto diviners: but as for thee, the LORD thy God hath not suffered thee so to do."*

(Isaiah 8:19) *"And when they say to you, 'Seek those who are mediums and wizards, who whisper and mutter,' should not a people seek their God? Should they seek the dead on behalf of the* *living?"*

(Exodus 20:4) *"Thou shalt not make unto thee any graven image, or any likeness of anything that is in heaven above, or that is in the earth beneath, or that is in the water under the earth."*

(Leviticus 20:6-8) *"And the soul that turneth after such as have familiar spirits, and after wizards, to go a whoring after them, I will even set my face against that soul, and will cut him off from among his people. Sanctify yourselves therefore, and be ye holy: for I am the LORD your God. And ye shall keep my statutes, and do them: I am the LORD which sanctify you."*

(Daniel 2:1) *"Now in the second year of Nebuchadnezzar's reign, Nebuchadnezzar had dreams; and his spirit was so troubled that his sleep left him. Then the king gave the command to call the magicians, the astrologers, the sorcerers, and the Chaldeans to tell the king his dreams. So they came and stood before the king... Daniel 5:47 The king answered Daniel, and said, 'Truly your God is the God of gods, the Lord of kings, and a revealer of secrets, since you could reveal this secret.'"*

The pursuit of knowledge is a testament to the human spirit's unending curiosity and its relentless drive to find meaning and purpose in life. Why on earth would a believer seek the occult for guidance?

(Psalm 119:104-105) *"Through Thy precepts I get understanding: therefore, I hate every false way. Thy word is a lamp unto my feet, and a light unto my path."*

14. Obedience and Submission to God:

True believers are compliant with orders from the Holy Spirit. When we obey the Holy Spirit's instructions and directions, it shows God that we truly trust Him, are listening to what He is saying, and have made Him Lord of our lives. Obedience is acting on what the Holy Spirit has said.

(John 14:23) *"Jesus answered and said unto him, If a man love me, he will obey my words: and my Father will love him, and we will come unto him, and make our abode with him."*

(1 Samuel 15:22) *"And Samuel said, Hath the LORD as great delight in burnt offerings and sacrifices, as in obeying the voice of the LORD? Behold, to obey is better than sacrifice, and to hearken than the fat of rams."*

(Deuteronomy 27:10) *"Thou shalt therefore obey the voice of the LORD thy God, and do His commandments and His statutes, which I command thee this day."*

The Grave Dangers of Counterfeit Christianity The Perilous Path: Unmasking the Dangers of Counterfeit Christianity

Why You Should Avoid the Risks and Pitfalls of Living as a Counterfeit Christian:

1. **Eternal Separation**: If left unchecked, counterfeit Christianity can lead to eternal separation from the Lord, resulting in spending eternity in hell.

   (Matthew 7:18-23) *"A good tree cannot bring forth evil fruit, neither can a corrupt tree bring forth good fruit. Every tree that bringeth not forth good fruit is hewn down, and cast into the fire. Wherefore by their fruits ye shall know them. Not everyone that saith unto me, Lord, Lord, shall enter into the kingdom of heaven; but he that doeth the will of my Father which is in heaven. Many will say to me in that day, Lord, Lord, have we not prophesied in thy name? and in thy name have cast out devils? and in thy name done many wonderful works? And then will I profess unto them, I never knew you: depart from me, ye that work iniquity."*

2. **Lack of Security**: Living as a counterfeit Christian opens the door to Satan and his angels, leaving you without divine protection.

[44]

(Psalm 9:1-3) *"He that dwelleth in the secret place of the most High shall abide under the shadow of the Almighty. I will say of the LORD, He is my refuge and my fortress: my God; in Him will I trust. Surely He shall deliver thee from the snare of the fowler, and from the noisome pestilence. He shall cover thee with His feathers, and under His wings shalt thou trust: His truth shall be thy shield and buckler."*

(Psalm 27:5) *"For in the time of trouble He shall hide me in His pavilion: in the secret of His tabernacle shall He hide me; He shall set me up upon a rock."* *(Proverbs 18:10) "The name of the LORD is a strong tower: the righteous runneth into it, and is safe."*

3. **Misleading Others**: Counterfeit Christians can mislead others about the true nature of faith, potentially damaging their perception and experience of Christianity. A counterfeit believer is a harm to other Christians, both in and out of the church, much like a bad apple that can spoil the whole bunch. The Word of God instructs us to be cautious of the company we keep.

    (2 Timothy 3:1-6) *"This know also, that in the last days perilous times shall come. For men shall be lovers of their own selves, covetous, boasters, proud, blasphemers, disobedient to parents, unthankful, unholy, Without natural affection, trucebreakers, false accusers, incontinent, fierce, despisers of those that are good, traitors, heady,* *highminded, lovers of pleasures more than lovers of God; Having a form of godliness, but denying the power thereof: from such turn away. For of this sort are they which creep into houses, and lead captive silly women laden with sins, led away with divers lusts, ever learning, and never able to come to the knowledge of the truth. Now as Jannes and Jambres withstood Moses, so do these also resist the truth: men of corrupt minds, reprobate concerning the faith. But they shall proceed no further: for their folly shall be manifest unto all men, as theirs also was."*

(Isaiah 5:20-21) *"Woe to those who call evil good and good evil, who turn darkness to light and light to darkness, who replace bitter with sweet and sweet with bitter. Woe to those who are wise in their own eyes and clever in their own sight."*

(Titus 1:16) *"They profess that they know God; but in works they deny Him, being abominable, and disobedient, and unto every good work reprobate."*

(Isaiah 29:13) *"Wherefore the Lord said, Forasmuch as this people draw near me with their mouth, and with their lips do honour me, but have removed their heart far from me, and their fear toward me is taught by the precept of men."*

4. **Counterfeit Believers Can Disguise Themselves as Apostles of Christ**: Counterfeit believers are knowingly deceitful workers who disguise themselves as apostles or followers of Christ.

[46]

(2 Corinthians 11:12-15) *"But what I do, that I will do, that I may cut off occasion from them which desire occasion; that wherein they glory, they may be found even as we. For such are false apostles, deceitful workers, transforming themselves into the apostles of Christ. And no marvel; for Satan himself is transformed into an angel of light. Therefore it is no great thing if his ministers also be transformed as the ministers of righteousness; whose end shall be according to their works."*

(Matthew 7:15-20) *"Beware of false prophets, which come to you in sheep's clothing, but inwardly they are ravening wolves. Ye shall know them by their fruits. Do men gather grapes of thorns, or figs of thistles? Even so every good tree bringeth forth good fruit; but a corrupt tree bringeth forth evil fruit. A good tree cannot bring forth evil fruit, neither can a corrupt tree bring forth good fruit. Every tree that bringeth not forth good fruit is hewn down, and cast into the fire. Wherefore by their fruits ye shall know them."*

(Romans 16:17-18) *"Now I beseech you, brethren, mark them which cause divisions and offences contrary to the doctrine which ye have learned; and avoid them. For they that are such serve not our Lord Jesus Christ, but their own belly; and by good words and fair speeches deceive the hearts of the simple. For your obedience is come abroad unto all men. I am glad therefore on your behalf: but yet I would have you wise unto that which is good, and simple* *concerning evil."*

5. **Loss of Integrity**: Living a double life can erode personal integrity and trustworthiness. Eventually, the truth tends to surface, damaging relationships and reputations. The Bible speaks extensively about integrity and the consequences of lacking it:

(Proverbs 10:9) *"He that walketh uprightly walketh surely: but he that perverteth his ways shall be known." This verse highlights that integrity leads to security, while deceit leads to exposure and trouble. As the elders say, "What's done in the dark will come into the light."*

(Proverbs 28:6) *"Better is the poor that walketh in his uprightness, than he that is perverse in his ways, though he be rich." This emphasizes that integrity is more valuable than wealth, and those who lose it, regardless of their material success, ultimately lack true worth.*

(Proverbs 11:3) *"The integrity of the upright guides them, but the crookedness of the treacherous destroys them." Here, the Bible warns that a lack of integrity leads to destruction, whereas integrity guides and sustains the upright.*

(Psalm 41:12) *"And as for me, thou upholdest me in mine integrity, and settest me before thy face forever." This verse shows that God values integrity and blesses those who maintain it.*

These passages underscore that living with integrity is crucial for a secure, valuable, and blessed life. Losing integrity, on the other hand, leads to exposure, destruction, and a lack of true guidance.

6. **Spiritual Emptiness**: Without genuine faith, there is a deep sense of spiritual hollowness. This can lead to a lack of fulfillment and constant inner turmoil. The Bible discusses spiritual emptiness and the need for a fulfilling relationship with God in several passages:

   (Psalm 42:1-2) *"As the hart panteth after the water brooks, so panteth my soul after thee, O God. My soul thirsteth for God, for the living God: when shall I come and appear before God?"* David was illustrating a deep longing for God, highlighting the emptiness that can be felt without Him.

   (Matthew 5:6) *"Blessed are they which do hunger and thirst after righteousness: for they shall be filled."* Here, Jesus speaks to the fulfillment that comes from seeking God and His righteousness. If you find yourself empty, thirsty, in a dry place, seek God, and like the woman at the well, you will never thirst again.

   (John 4:13-14) *"Jesus answered, 'But whosoever drinketh of the water that I shall give him shall never thirst; but the water that I shall give him shall be in him a well of water springing up into everlasting life.'"* Jesus contrasts physical thirst with the spiritual fulfillment only He can provide.

   These passages highlight the significance of seeking a

deep, authentic relationship with God to fill the spiritual void. Anything less leads to a persistent sense of emptiness and dissatisfaction. You'll never fill it with sports, shopping, social media posts, or people—only God can fill these voids. Try Him.

7. **Hypocrisy**: Being a counterfeit Christian involves preaching one thing while practicing and living another. This hypocrisy will lead to guilt and shame. The Bible has strong words about hypocrisy:

(Matthew 23:27-28) *"Jesus said, 'Woe unto you, scribes and Pharisees, hypocrites! For ye are like unto whited sepulchres, which indeed appear beautiful outward, but are within full of dead men's bones, and of all uncleanness. Even so ye also outwardly appear righteous unto men, but within ye are full of hypocrisy and iniquity.'"* Jesus condemns religious leaders who focus on outward appearances rather than inner righteousness, hindering the growth of men and Kingdom living.

(Matthew 7:5) *"Thou hypocrite, first cast out the beam out of thine own eye; and then shalt thou see clearly to cast out the mote out of thy brother's eye."* This verse points to the importance of self-examination and addressing one's own flaws before criticizing others.

(Isaiah 29:13) *"Wherefore the Lord said, 'Forasmuch as this people draw near me with their mouth, and with their lips do* *honour me, but have removed their heart far from me, and their fear toward me is taught by the precept of men.'"* God desires genuine devotion from believers rather than empty rituals and lip service. The Bible repeatedly calls out hypocrisy and emphasizes the need for authentic, inner transformation rather than mere outward displays of faith.

8. **Self-Deception**: Pretending to be devout might lead to self-deception, making it difficult to recognize one's own need for true spiritual growth and transformation. The Bible has strong warnings against self-deception:

(James 1:22-23) *"But be ye doers of the word, and not hearers only, deceiving your own selves. For if any be a hearer of the word, and not a doer, he is like unto a man beholding his natural face in a glass."* This verse highlights the importance of aligning actions with beliefs, avoiding the pitfall of deceiving oneself by mere hearing without demonstration and action.

(Jeremiah 17:9) *"The heart is deceitful above all things, and desperately wicked: who can know it?"* This points to the human heart's capacity for self-deception, emphasizing the need for divine insight and the importance of self-examination.

(Galatians 6:3-5) *"For if a man think himself to be something, when he is nothing, he deceiveth himself. But let every man prove his own work, and then shall he have* *rejoicing in himself alone, and not in another. For every man shall bear his own burden."* This verse underscores the danger of pride and overestimating one's righteousness without God.

(Proverbs 30:12) *"There is a generation that are pure in their own eyes, and yet is not washed from their filthiness."* This warns against blindness to one's own flaws and the need for true purification. In their eyes, they see no need for a savior or forgiveness for sins since they have none to confess.

These scriptures call for introspection, humility, and a commitment to genuine self-awareness and integrity to avoid the dangers of self-deception.

9. **Lack of True Support**: Without a genuine spiritual community, counterfeit Christians may miss out on meaningful support and guidance from authentic believers. The Bible emphasizes the importance of genuine support from a spiritual community and highlights the consequences of its absence:

(Hebrews 10:24-25) *"And let us consider one another to provoke unto love and to good works: Not forsaking the assembling of ourselves together, as the manner of some is; but exhorting one another: and so much the more, as ye see the day approaching."* This verse stresses the need for regular fellowship and mutual encouragement. Do you have a church home? If not, may I ask why? The Bible emphasizes the importance of having one for your spiritual well-being.

(Galatians 6:2) *"Bear ye one another's burdens, and so fulfill the law of Christ."* A true spiritual community is one where members help bear each other's burdens, reflecting Christ's love. This is why your church attendance is so important—not just for you, but for the person next to you who may need your love and support to carry them through. Yes, online services are a great tool if you are unable to attend in person, but there is nothing like the human contact and support found in a physical gathering. God made this a request, not a suggestion, because He knows the profound impact of being part of a loving, supportive community.

(1 Thessalonians 5:11*)* *"Wherefore comfort yourselves together, and edify one another, even as also ye do."* Encouragement and edification are key elements of a supportive, Godly community.

(Ecclesiastes 4:9-10) *"Two are better than one; because they have a good reward for their labour. For if they fall, the one will lift up his fellow: but woe to him that is alone when he falleth; for he hath not another to help him up."* This emphasizes the strength and support found in companionship. My heart goes out to those who haven't had the opportunity to form meaningful friendships. The absence of such connections can leave a void that is deeply felt. True friendships provide support, joy, and a sense of belonging that enriches our lives in countless ways.

Without them, individuals may miss out on the shared experiences and emotional bonds that make life truly fulfilling.

With deep gratitude, I extend my heartfelt thanks to all my prayer warriors and partners. Your prayers sustained me when my mom was on life support and kept me in remembrance of God's healing and miraculous powers. Your support guided me through my own physical and spiritual challenges. Some of you offered correction and tough love, and for that, I am profoundly grateful. Thank you for being there for me as we do life together.

If you have no friends, associates, or prayer partners, the Bible offers this advice: **(Proverbs 18:24)** *"A man that hath friends must shew himself friendly."* How about working on being friendly if you are not?

These dangers highlight the importance of authenticity and integrity in one's spiritual journey. A lack of true support from a spiritual community can lead to isolation, discouragement, and spiritual stagnation. Genuine fellowship is vital for spiritual growth, accountability, and mutual encouragement.

When examining your relationship with the Lord, ask yourself if you are living authentically. Here are some tips for self-examination:

- **Seek His Presence**: An authentic relationship with Christ means your heart longs for His presence and you strive to live righteously.

- **Evaluate Your Response to Sin**: If sin does not repulse you, take a moment to examine your heart.

- **Assess Your Speech**: If you find yourself cursing people out or giving them a piece of your mind impulsively, it's time to reflect on your heart's condition.

- **Consider Your Habits**: Strive to approach life with a compassionate and mindful heart. In the Bible, being "sober-minded" (1 Peter 5:8) is described as maintaining a clear, disciplined, and self-controlled focus, enabling one to navigate challenges with wisdom and grace.

- **Watch the company you keep. (2Corinthians 6:14-17)** Be ye not unequally yoked together with unbelievers: for what fellowship hath righteousness with unrighteousness? and what communion hath light with darkness? And what concord hath Christ with Belial? or what part hath he that believeth with an infidel? And what agreement hath the temple of God with idols? for ye are the temple of the living God; as God hath said, I will dwell in them, and walk in *them*; and I will be their God, and they shall be my people. Wherefore come out from among them, and be ye separate, saith the Lord, and touch not the unclean *thing*; and I will receive you.....

The End of Days: A Tale of Reflection on Faith and Time for a False Believer:

For Marcus, Sunday mornings held a special kind of serenity. It was a time when the world seemed to slow down, and the usual hustle of life gave way to a peaceful quietude. His favorite breakfast spot became a sanctuary, where the clinking of cutlery and the soft murmur of the few early risers blended into a symphony of solitude.

During these moments, Marcus found himself in deep contemplation. He wrestled with the guilt of a small lie to his grandmother—a lie that spoke volumes about his current state of belief. The church, once a cornerstone of his upbringing, now felt like a distant memory, a tradition he could no longer reconcile with his scientific pursuits.

As an engineer, Marcus's world was governed by the laws of physics and the tangible evidence of theories proven true. The concept of faith, so integral to his grandmother and the community he grew up in, now seemed elusive. It wasn't that he had renounced his faith, but rather that he was on a quest for his own truth—a set of beliefs that he could reconcile with his understanding of the universe and his engineering passions.

Sunday mornings were still sacred for many, but for Marcus, they no longer revolved around sermons or worship. His ritual now consisted of a spinach omelet and big, fluffy blueberry pancakes at his favorite breakfast spot, followed by a few hours spent washing and waxing his pride and joy—a sleek, new 5.0 Mustang. His "Sunday service" was a bucket of soapy water and a shining coat of polish on the Mustang's flawless candy apple red finish.

Marcus had grown tired of the constant talk about the end of days, of God's judgment, and the apocalypse—all preached with fervor by his grandmother and echoed in the walls of the church. He had spent too many hours in those pews, and now he was ready to live life on his own terms.

"I'm young," he often reminded himself, "I've got plenty of time to figure out if this God thing is real or not."

That was his mantra, and he repeated it every Sunday, as if to reassure himself that the luxury of time was still on his side. But this morning—this surreal morning—his usual comfort routine felt hollow.

His grandmother's warnings about the end of days echoed in his mind as he stared blankly at the TV screens, watching reports of worldwide catastrophes. The apocalyptic stories that had once seemed so far-fetched, the ones he had dismissed with a casual wave, were now unfolding right before his eyes. It was happening, and he knew it.

Suddenly, his Sunday wasn't about the Mustang, pancakes, or whether he'd meet up with friends later. It was about survival. It was about the terrifying possibility that he had run out of time.

For Marcus, this day had felt like any other, with the sun glowing and the birds serenading the morning with their cheerful chirps. The world seemed at peace, and the simple joy of a sunny day was enough to lift the spirits of anyone who stepped outside. But as quickly as the light appeared, it vanished, replaced by an ominous darkness that silenced the birds and brought an eerie chill to the air.

As the rain began to fall, the television in the local diner, usually tuned to the anticipation of the week's big football game, displayed a stream of breaking news that captured everyone's attention. Reports of an earthquake in the Middle East surfaced, with significant tremors felt across the region. A hurricane, having just made landfall in Hawaii, was casting its shadow over the islands, leaving a trail of destruction in its wake.

And then, the most baffling of all—several planes had inexplicably fallen from the sky, and several cruise ships had run amok, leaving experts and laypeople alike scratching their heads in confusion and fear. The newscasters, usually the harbingers of calm and information, could only speculate about the world's end as the series of disasters unfolded.

What was going on? The day had started so beautifully, so full of promise. Given the circumstances, Marcus could only wonder if this was the apocalypse his grandma and Pastor Uncle Willie had constantly referred to. *I hope that's not the case. Since I haven't devoted my life to Christ, I am unprepared. I thought I had more time,* he pondered. Since he was a little boy in church, the old folks always talked about the end of days, and now it seemed to be here. What should he do?

Marcus stood at the crossroads of uncertainty, his mind racing with the teachings of his childhood. The end of days—a concept so often discussed by the elder members of his family—now felt like a tangible reality. The world around him seemed to echo with signs of tumultuous times, and Marcus found himself grappling with a sense of urgency he had never known before.

As a child, Marcus had listened intently to the stories of revelation and redemption, of trials and tribulations that would signal the world's final chapter. His grandma's voice, laced with conviction, and Uncle Willie's impassioned sermons had painted vivid pictures of what was to come. Yet, in the hustle of daily life, those images had faded into the background, becoming distant echoes rather than immediate concerns.

Now, as Marcus faced the world's apparent unraveling, those echoes resounded with clarity. As Marcus listened intently to the news, the lessons of his youth surged forward, reminding him of the values and beliefs that had been instilled in him. The end of days was not just a prophecy but a call to action—a reminder to live a life of purpose, to cherish each moment, and to embrace faith as a guiding light.

Marcus now realized he had been living as a counterfeit believer. The cup he gripped so tightly in his hand, and the blood that ran down his hand, caught the attention of no one in the diner. Those who were left behind with Marcus all had the life drained from their faces.

As if the news hadn't already shaken him to his core, what happened next made the hair on Marcus's neck stand on end. The TV revealed something so chilling it froze him in place. He gripped the glass in his hand until it shattered, spilling his drink across the table, drenching his shirt and pants. The restaurant's TVs were all tuned to the same story—a bizarre, unexplainable event. Millions of people around the world had suddenly vanished without a trace.

The story played out on every screen, but Marcus didn't need the news to tell him what was happening. He had heard this tale all his life from his grandmother, a story that had felt like a distant, impossible legend—until now. He sat paralyzed in the booth, a spot that once seemed perfect for a family of four but now felt unbearably lonely, occupied by a single man trying to enjoy a simple breakfast special.

As people murmured and debated the phenomenon around him, Marcus knew the terrifying truth. His instincts screamed at him to call his grandmother, to reach out to his uncle—anyone—but the sheer terror of what was unfolding left him frozen, unable to move. The truth settled over him like a suffocating weight.

Marcus fled to his Mustang, seeking solace and refuge. A blood-curdling scream erupted from the depths of his soul, a raw expression of his anguish. He had been left behind. The true believers had vanished, leaving the world in disarray. His eyes fixed on the diamond-studded cross air freshener hanging from the rearview mirror—a stark reminder of his counterfeit faith. The chaos outside mirrored the turmoil within him as he grappled with the reality of his spiritual emptiness.

The bill had come due for Marcus. The consequence of his choice to live as a counterfeit believer weighed heavily upon him. The repercussions of his actions were now unavoidable, like a dark cloud looming over his soul. Each decision, each moment of insincerity, had accumulated into a debt that demanded payment. The reality of his spiritual emptiness and the facade he had maintained for so long now confronted him with undeniable force. The cost of living a life devoid of true faith and authenticity had finally caught up with him, and there was no escaping the reckoning of being *Left Behind*.

Sharing Salvation with Faith, Love and Care

Salvation means being saved from separation from God. According to the Bible, all mankind—both men and women—inherit this separation because of Adam's disobedience in the Garden of Eden. This act of sin brought spiritual death and separation from God into the world. But in His mercy, God desired for us to spend eternity in Heaven with Him. His love for us was so great that He sent His only Son, Jesus, to end that separation and legally restore our relationship with Him, just as it was before Adam sinned. This restored relationship with God is a free gift.

False Believer, now is the time to truly examine your

heart. If you need to repent, do so NOW!

- **Luke 13:3**: *"I tell you, Nay: but, except ye repent, ye shall all likewise perish."*

- **2 Peter 3:9**: *"The Lord is not slow in keeping His promise, as some understand slowness, but is patient with you, not wanting anyone to perish but everyone to come to repentance."*

- **Revelation 2:5**: *"Therefore, keep in mind how far you have fallen. Repent and perform the deeds you did at first. But if you do not repent, I will come to you and remove your lampstand from its place."*

What is Salvation and Why is it Important?

Salvation, in Christian belief, is the deliverance from sin and its consequences, granted by God's grace through faith in Jesus Christ. It's the ultimate rescue—a bridge from spiritual death to eternal life.

Salvation is important because it addresses the core problem of human existence: separation from God due to sin. Here's why it matters:

1. Restored Relationship: Salvation restores the broken relationship between humans and God, bringing reconciliation and peace.

2. Eternal Life: It promises eternal life with God, as opposed to eternal separation, which is often described as spiritual death or damnation.

3. Transformation: Salvation transforms lives, bringing new purpose, hope, and moral direction. It marks the beginning of a new life in Christ, characterized by growth and transformation.

4. Freedom from Sin: It delivers believers from the power and penalty of sin, offering forgiveness and freedom.

5. Grace and Mercy: Salvation highlights God's grace and mercy, showcasing His love and desire for all to be saved and come to know the truth.

In essence, salvation is central to the Christian faith because it's the pathway to spiritual renewal and eternal communion with God. It's the foundation of hope and the reason for the transformative power of Christianity in believers' lives.

CONCLUSION

This book was born from a deep, introspective question that has lingered in the hearts of many: Why are there so many hypocritical people in the church? Driven by a desire to seek answers and uncover the truth, Pastor Joe dedicated nearly six months to this crucial topic during our Saturday Bible Study sessions. Through countless hours of discussion, reflection, and scripture study, we gathered invaluable insights and teachings.

From the extensive notes, sermons, and scriptures provided by Pastor Joe, I felt compelled to compile this book. Our mission was to shed light on the complexities of hypocrisy within the church and to provide guidance for fostering a more authentic and sincere Christian community. We wrote this book to encourage introspection, understanding, and growth, ultimately striving to strengthen the bonds of faith and integrity among believers.

The deeper we explored this profound subject, the more we recognized the urgent need to share our discoveries with others. We felt a deep responsibility to extend our knowledge and help prevent the dangers of living a counterfeit Christian life. Imagine having the keys, tools, knowledge, understanding, and the power of God within you to save a drowning person. How could we possibly withhold such life-saving wisdom? We invite you to share this book with others, so together we can be effective witnesses and bring the transformative power of faith to those who need it most. Let's spread this crucial message and make a positive impact on the lives of many.

Prayer of Salvation:

Dear God, I come to You in the name of Your Son Jesus. After reading this, I realize why I need salvation. I ask You to forgive me of my sin, which I inherited from Adam. You said that the wages of sin are death—eternal death and separation from You. BUT, the gift of God is eternal life through Jesus Christ. And You said if I confess with my mouth that Jesus is Lord, and if I acknowledge that He died to restore my relationship with You—while believing in my heart that You raised Jesus from the dead—I will be saved (Romans 6:23; 10:9). Right now, I confess aloud that Jesus is Lord, and I believe in my heart that You raised Him from the dead for me. Thank You for saving me! I believe these things are true and that You hear my prayer.

In Jesus' name I pray, Amen.

A True Child of God Cannot Continue to Habitually Practice Sin!

[66]